How To Improve Your Social Skills

Ultimate Tatics To Maximize Your Conversation Skills in a Day

By: Crystal Stevens

Introduction

I want to thank you and congratulate you for downloading the book, *"How To Improve Your Social Skills: Ultimate Tatics To Maximize Your Conversation Skills in a Day"*.

This book contains proven steps and strategies on how to overcome your fear of communicating and socializing with other people and level up your social skills. Hey, I'm not judging. We've all been there at some point in our lives. Even I used to be this shy, soft-spoken person who doesn't want to mingle with other people in the crowd.

However, as time goes by, I realized that social situations will always be there, no matter where I hide and how fast I avoid them. In this book, I'll be sharing with you the personal techniques that I helped me conquer my insecurities in terms of engaging with another human being. From coming up with interesting conversation piece to developing self-confidence, this book is packed with gems that you may have never heard before.

Whether you are looking for courage to ask someone out on a date or you need tenacity to be able to deliver a speech on public, this book will help you maximize your conversation skills and level up the way you communicate with other people.

So, are you ready to unlock a new skill? If your answer is yes, then you are on the right track, my friend.

Again, thank you for downloading this book. I hope you enjoy it!

© **Copyright 2019 by Crystal Stevens - All rights reserved.**

This document is geared towards providing reliable information based on studies and research in regards to the topic and issue covered. Any information or advice given within this book may change overtime. The author will not be held reliable for any action or results that the reader may decide to take upon the given information. The publication is sold with the idea that the publisher is not required to render accounting, officially permitted, or otherwise, qualified services. If advice is necessary, legal or professional, a practiced individual in the profession should be ordered.

- From a Declaration of Principles which was accepted and approved equally by a Committee of the American Bar Association and a Committee of Publishers and Associations.

In no way is it legal to reproduce, duplicate, or transmit any part of this document in either electronic means or in printed format. Recording of this publication is strictly prohibited and any storage of this document is not allowed unless with written permission from the publisher. All rights reserved.

The information provided herein is stated to be truthful and consistent, in that any liability, in terms of inattention or otherwise, by any usage or abuse of any policies, processes, or directions contained within is the solitary and utter responsibility of the recipient reader. Under no circumstances will any legal responsibility or blame be held against the publisher for any reparation, damages, or monetary loss due to the information herein, either directly or indirectly.

Respective authors own all copyrights not held by the publisher.

The information herein is offered for informational purposes solely, and is universal as so. The presentation of the information is without contract or any type of guarantee assurance.

The trademarks that are used are without any consent, and the publication of the trademark is without permission or backing by the trademark owner. All trademarks and brands within this book are for clarifying purposes only and are the owned by the owners themselves, not affiliated with this document.

Chapter 1: Social Situations are Everywhere

Social situations can be a little overwhelming at times. This is a fact I've learned to accept as I was growing up. You meet different kinds of people, expecting you to behave in a way that is acceptable to society. Otherwise, you will unsolicited judgement or criticism that may or may not affect how you see yourself.

This is why there are a lot of people who would rather stay secluded in the comfort of their own home just to avoid the uneasiness of a social interaction. If you are one of those people who do not feel comfortable interacting with others, you may have felt at one point that you are missing out on all the potential fun, learning, and growth that you should be experiencing if you just go out and socialize.

Do you often miss out on social events because you are not comfortable interacting with other people? Would you rather choose to lock yourself in your bedroom than socialize? Would you rather spend all day reading or doing solitary activities such as playing video games than accept any invitation to go outside with friends? If your answer to all these questions is yes, then you are not alone.

Many people feel the same way. Even I used to be in your shoes a long time ago, that's why I understand what you're going through right now. I know the feeling of discomfort, awkwardness, or sometimes fear that creeps inside the skin and down the spine whenever you find yourself in the middle of social situations. I'm also familiar with that voice inside the head, telling you to run away as fast as you can.

But that was a long time ago. As time goes by, I realized that I can never truly avoid being in the middle of social situations. It's part of life. After all, we are social beings created to interact and communicate with each other. So, instead of running away, I gradually accepted it and learned to deal with it. It wasn't instant though. It took me some time to overcome my shyness and improve my social skills at a level that I've become comfortable talking to other people, sharing my thoughts, and simply being a normal human being who knows how to engage in typical conversations.

I know that this is your goal, too — to get to that point where interacting with other people feels natural and comfortable; where you don't need to force yourself to communicate or put so much effort into speaking out your thoughts. You will get there. I promise you. If I did it, so will you. And I will help you along the way. The tips and tricks I shared in this book will serve as your daily guide and reminder that everything is possible. As long as you follow the steps religiously, you will be able to maximize your conversation skills in no time.

Now, before going into the details on how to improve your social skills, it is important to keep in mind that being shy is not a negative trait. Do not put yourself down for being the kind of person who, at this point, doesn't want to socialize with other people.

However, I want you to know that socialization is an important and inevitable part of life.

Why Socialization is Important

Whether you think you need to socialize or not, it is undeniable that you cannot entirely avoid being around other people. Certain everyday situations require you to go out and interact with others. School and work are some of the most common places where you will be required to be around other people. So unless you do not need to learn anything in school or you don't need a job to earn money, you really have to sharpen those social skills.

Despite being unavoidable, socialization can help you build a network that would help you achieve your goals. In most of your endeavors, you will need certain people to support and help you. Whether you are looking for a certain service or product, or getting a job done, you can always rely on some people in your network to help you.

Furthermore, you can't find a person to share your important moments with if you typically hide away in the comfort of your home. Going on a date to find a partner or attending social gatherings to meet some friends would be impossible if you choose to withdraw from social situations.

Aside from the tangible benefits of having other people in your life as a result of socialization, having a close network of friends that you trust have a lot of psychological and emotional benefits as well. For one thing, it gives you the feeling of belongingness and acceptance — like being part of a community, a church group, or a support group.

For a lot of people, this sense of acceptance can help fight off depressive tendencies. Having friends can serve as a distraction from feeling something hurtful since you get to have other people with whom you can spend time. It also helps you feel loved and cared for because you have a network that will listen to you and support you no matter what your plans are in life. Furthermore, having a network of friends can help you build your confidence and help you feel better about yourself.

Social Anxiety, Introversion, or Just Weak Social Skills?

Before we begin with the tips and exercises that will help improve your social skills in no time, it is important to first point out what may be causing the discomfort that you feel when you are engaging in a social situation.

When confronted by an overwhelming social situation, like if you start to feel your cheeks are flushing, your heart is beating fast, you feel weak and you start to tremble, you sweat profusely, you feel nauseous, you can't breath properly, your muscles start to feel tensed, you feel a sort of lightheadedness and your mind goes blank, then you may be feeling the physiological indicators of social anxiety.

Social anxiety, depending on its severity, can be diagnosed as a clinical disorder that requires a mental health professional in order to be treated. The difference between plain shyness and social anxiety disorder is that the latter may cause significant disruption in a person's everyday life because of the fear of social situations.

Social anxiety disorder may prompt the patient to feel intense fear and discomfort to the point that he or she will avoid social activities like work, school, or even family gatherings to alleviate the discomfort.

Other symptoms of social anxiety are psychological. People with the disorder often fear being judged in situations involving talking to strangers, being humiliated or embarrassed, appearing to look noticeably nervous, and being the center of attention.

However, it is very normal for you to feel some of these symptoms even if you do not have social anxiety disorder. Maybe you feel these physiological and psychological symptoms but not to an intense degree that you will leave your job or your studies to be a recluse. Also, you may only have a specific social situation that really causes you severe anxiety, such as dating or going to parties. You may just be an introvert, which explains why you sometimes prefer your own company than having others. Or, maybe you just have underdeveloped or rusty social skills due to the lack of proper human interactions in your life or various other reasons.

Social anxiety disorder is very different from being an introvert.

Introversion is a personality trait that involves having an internal focus. An introvert is stimulated by his or her own thoughts, emotions, and mood; thus, he or she no longer needs to find stimulation from other people. Some psychologists explain that introversion does not equate to being shy. Introverts can be sociable in a lot of cases, but being in a social situation depletes their energy. They simply need some time alone to recuperate their energy; thus, they tend to require a few days to be alone with their own thoughts. They prefer solitary activities that involve no other person.

Despite being often confused and interchanged, introversion differs from shyness. Schmidt and Buss, researchers from the University of Texas, reported that even though both refer to social withdrawal, introversion refers to the "lack of interest to be in a social situation", whereas shyness is the "fear and discomfort felt when in a social situation that results in inhibited behavior and sometimes social withdrawal".

There are studies that look at how introversion and shyness correlate, and some studies suggest that being an introvert may hinder the development of social skills of children due to the lack of social interaction, making them more shy as they grow older into adolescence and adulthood.

There are a lot of self-proclaimed shy people who excel in jobs where only the highly sociable are expected to succeed. For instance, John F. Kennedy was once described as being a "very introverted man" who keeps to himself most of the time. A lot of well-known celebrities have attested to being shy such as Johnny Depp who said, "I'm living, in a sense, like a fugitive. I don't like to be in social situations", or Kim Kardashian who said "I'm the girl who's too shy to dance in a nightclub. The real Kim is very shy and reserved and not outspoken and loud".

There are many others just like them who overcame their shyness by facing their fears of social situation in order for them to achieve their life objectives. They did not let their shyness rule their reality.

We all experience some sort of anxiety in some way, and social events where you are expected to interact with other people can be a bit overwhelming at times. You just have to have the right mindset and prepare yourself so that you will always know what to say and how to behave despite being shy.

So whether you are shy, or an introvert with weak social skills, or for any other reason that you are reading this book, congratulations in taking the first step! This means that you have decided to step up and beat your own weakness. I will share with you ultimate strategies and proven techniques in improving your social skills and develop that confidence to speak up and be heard.

* * * * *

CHAPTER SUMMARY:

- We cannot avoid social situations. They're part of life and at one point or another, you will find yourself in a position where you have to interact with other people.

- Socialization is important. After all, we are social beings created to communicate with one another. Socialization serves as an opportunity for growth and learning. Moreover, it provides a sense belongingness and acceptance, having friends and people around us who support us in what we do.

- Social anxiety is a clinical disorder that requires help from mental health professional. This condition may cause nauseousness, feeling of weakness, rapid beating of the heart, improper breathing, and other health concerns due to an overwhelming feeling of facing a social situation.

- Introversion, on the other hand, is a personality trait characterized by focusing on yourself. You are considered an introvert if you are stimulated by your own thoughts, emotions, or mood, and you don't need stimulation from other people.

- Another reason you may feel discomfort, awkwardness, or fear towards social interactions is having weak or underdeveloped social skills. Whatever the reason is, you can successfully overcome this problem by following the tips, tricks, and strategies outlined in the succeeding chapters of this book.

Chapter 2: Read More, Learn More, Talk More

One of the reasons why shy people choose to withdraw from social situations is the fear of humiliating themselves. They fear that they might say something stupid and they might get questioned or, worse, laughed at. They also feel uneasy entering a social situation where they have nothing substantial to say.

Does this sound familiar to you? Do you feel this way most of the times?

If this is the reason why you avoid social situations, then the key to banishing the fear is to be prepared. Just like getting into a battle, have your weapons of attack ready with you at all times.

Of course, you will never know which topics of conversation would be useful for every social situation, that's why it will be helpful if you are well-read in various topics. The more you read, the more ideas and information you can store in your head in case a sudden social situation comes up.

Reading can help you prepare for socialization. It will give you interesting topics to talk about when you start a conversation with a boss, colleague, a hot date, or strangers in the bus stop. Reading the newspaper is a safe way to stock up on topics that most people will find interesting in most social groups. Current events in the local community and even in the global scale are things that most people have something to say about. You can open up a topic of conversation from an interesting news event and other people will weigh in on their opinions and ideas.

The newspaper offers a vast range of topics that any person you come across will find interesting. You can read up about business news, fashion trends, politics, global events, sports, health, and lifestyle. You can have all these topics in your arsenal to prepare you in a social event where there are different people interested in various topics. However, for casual conversations, try to stick to the neutral, interesting, and light topics rather than going into a deep discussion or debate on controversial issues like politics or religion.

Furthermore, if you find yourself in social situations where you feel like you don't have anything to say or anyone to talk to, reading will help you feel more confident to join the conversation, if people around you are already talking about a current issue. You will never feel like a fool in a conversation if you always have something substantial to say.

A study published in Science Journal in 2013 also revealed that reading books can help improve your social skills by increasing your ability to empathize with other people or interpret a social situation based on limited cues. Reading literary fiction books sharpens your social perception and increases emotional intelligence, both of which are essential in effective communication and relationship building. Books are emotionally subtle compared to television and movies, thus making you think more. This allows you to practice making inferences regarding the social situation in what you are reading and think about what the characters are feeling.

If you're not really the type of person who is fond of reading, don't worry! Here are some easy steps you can slowly follow and practice to help you read more and gain the knowledge that you need to start conversations.

1. Read the headlines every morning.

Allot some time in the morning to read what is happening in the world. Instead of scrolling through social media without purpose, try opening the newspaper. If you are not fond of reading the paper, start by going through the headlines first, then read the articles that you find interesting.

Start reading for yourself and not for the purpose of impressing others. You will find it much more enjoyable if you read the topics that jump out of the page to you.

Once you get the habit of reading the headlines in the morning, you can start reading a few more details in the first few paragraphs of an article where most of the facts are presented. If you don't have a newspaper, scroll through the day's headlines using online applications in your phone. That does not sound too daunting, does it?

Remember, it takes regular routine to develop a habit. When you do this often, eventually, looking for the morning paper will be part of your morning habit.

2. Always carry a reading material with you.

You'll never know when you get stuck in a queue, when you have to wait for an appointment that is running late, or when you have to wait for your flight, your train, or a bus. Make the most of your idle time by cracking open that book, newspaper, or magazine. You'll find that it won't take too much of your time to read, especially if you maximize your down time.

Another upside is it reduces your stress level when you are waiting because your time is spent on something productive.

3. Start with shorter books.

Sure, it seems like a daunting task to finish a thick book with more than a thousand pages (and no pictures!). For a person who is not fond of reading or busy with other things, you'll start to think that you will never finish reading that book. So don't start with books that are intimidating. Try reading shorter novels, magazines, digests, or a book that is composed of a collection of short stories or essays.

If you really want to finish a thick book, give yourself a quota of maybe 30 pages per day. Dividing up the task into smaller and more manageable tasks will make it seem less intimidating.

4. Try audiobooks.

If you think reading a book is unproductive, because perhaps you're spending a lot of your time but not really finishing a lot of work, why not try listening to books instead? Yes, you can do this through the help of audiobooks.

You can listen to books and broaden your knowledge, even when you running on the treadmill, driving in your car, or even doing the laundry. This way you can be productive in your commute or house chores while learning new topics.

5. Allot a certain time of the day for reading.

It's hard to keep the habit of reading if you always have a lot of things to do during the day, that's why it is important to set a schedule and commit to it.

You can set 30 minutes of reading before going to sleep or after dinner. It does not seem much, but if you add up 30 minutes everyday, you can end up reading a lot more books than you think in a year.

The good thing is, most people who tend to shy away from social situations often choose to stay at home and reading is their solitary activity. If you are already reading a lot, then you are already prepared with the topics you can talk about.

But if you still don't feel like you're ready to go out and socialize, then the problem is not with how much conversation topics you know, but maybe with your confidence or motivation, which we will discuss in the next chapter.

*****

CHAPTER SUMMARY:

- To be ready to start or join in a conversation, you need to have broad knowledge about many things around you. In order to have this knowledge, you need to read books, newspapers, magazines, and other reading materials.

- Stay up to date with news and current events because these are common conversation starters. When you're equipped with the latest news or interesting information, you can be confident to start a conversation with your boss or join in a discussion that's already happening.

- For casual conversations, stick to the neutral, interesting topics rather than going into a deep discussion on controversial issues like politics or religion.

- If reading isn't part of your daily routine, there are several tips to help you read more. These include reading the newspaper every morning, carrying a reading material with you at all times, reading shorter books, listening to audiobooks, and sticking to a daily reading time.

Chapter 3: Level Up Your Self-Confidence

If you have been reading and keeping yourself updated about things that are going on around you, but are still riddled with fear about the thought of entering a social situation, then it's time to work on that confidence.

There are a lot of ways to stop feeling so awkward when you are around other people. You just have to defeat your insecurities and feel more confident about yourself. Here are some tips to make you more socially confident.

Build Your Confidence.

The first thing to keep in mind in building up your confidence is believing in yourself. I know, it sounds easier said than done. But here are some ways to get you to start feeling good about yourself and your social skills.

1. Stop the negative self-talk.

If you hear your brain saying thins like, "I can't do it", "I am awkward and shy", "I'll just end up saying something stupid", "They will laugh at me", or "I'll probably just stay in the corner and hope nobody talks to me", then you are simply feeding the insecurity monster inside your brain.

Stop talking to yourself or about yourself that depreciates your value.

If you keep thinking about yourself that way, then chances are, it will soon be your reality. It's called a self-fulfilling prophecy. It is nothing but a mere prediction based on no evidence, but the mere fact that you think it, will indirectly result to the actual fulfillment of what you are thinking.

Let's try to visualize it. You keep thinking, "They will all laugh at me". The moment you enter a social event, your negative thought will start to make you feel nervous. The nerves start to show, you feel flustered, your voice starts shaking, and you sweat profusely. A person may notice how nervous you look and they may actually start laughing. And it all started because of your one negative thought.

So banish the negative self-talk and be kinder to yourself. Think of all the positive things about you, and appreciate the qualities that you like about yourself. Practice positive affirmations and build yourself up. Stop deprecating yourself, and start appreciating what a wonderful person you are.

2. Accept yourself.

You have to first know yourself, before you can accept yourself. Maybe you are naturally shy or introverted or maybe you are an extrovert with poor social skills. Whatever the case is, you should try to figure out what the root cause of your anxiety is so you can address the problem with a more targeted strategy.

If your personality is shy or introverted, there is nothing to worry about. Having these personality traits are not negative things. It doesn't make you less of a human being just because you feel shy sometimes.

Being in any part of the introvert-extrovert continuum is neither positive nor negative; it is just simply what it is, and you have to accept yourself for who you are. If you can't accept yourself, then how do you expect other people to accept you?

3. Focus on yourself and not about impressing others.

It is important that you see yourself in a positive light. Soon, other people will see you the way you see yourself. If you keep labeling yourself as boring, then other people will receive that vibe coming from you and they may actually start to think you are boring.

Don't worry about appearing interesting to others. Instead, try to be someone whom you find interesting. If you are interested in your thoughts, your ideas, and yourself, the right people will be drawn to your positive energy.

One of the reasons why certain people are anxious about social situations is they care too much about what other people think of them. These people have high self-monitoring personality, wherein they alter their behavior and appearance in order to be liked by other people.

While this can be helpful in some ways and in moderation, being too concerned about being liked can be counterproductive for your social development. You tend to do the things that you think other people will approve of, but you end up neglecting what you like, and you get disappointed with yourself.

So talk about what makes you happy to the people who will find it interesting. Stop trying too hard to impress everyone. Engaging in a social interaction means entering a give-and-take exchange, so the pressure of being interesting is not entirely on you.

4. Level your expectations.

You can't please everyone, and that's okay.

You can't expect all people to accept you and like you. There will always be people out there who will not agree with you or reject you. But it does not mean that it is because of your inadequacy.

Just know that there are billions of people in the world and one rejection is nothing. It does not reflect on you, but mostly on them. They may be going through something difficult, or you are just simply incompatible in terms of ideas and interests.

Whatever the reason is, don't take social rejection too hard. There will always be people out there who will want to hear what you say, who will find your interests interesting, and who will respond positively to your social cues. You just have to find the right audience.

The spotlight effect is a psychological tendency that most people have, wherein they think that people around them are more focused and invested in them than they actually are. They tend to think that they are the center of everyone's attention, which is why they may feel self-conscious that people will notice their flaws or they will see how nervous they are.

The truth is, most people are focused on themselves and they will rarely notice a minor flaw. So stop thinking that everyone is looking at you; it will only make you feel more nervous. If you slip up or said something wrong, it's okay. Chances are, the people who heard you will not even remember what you said the next day.

Once you have completed the process of changing the way you think about and see yourself, the next step to gaining your self-confidence is to act like you are already confident.

Fake Your Confidence

It might sound negative, but what I meant by faking your confidence is to appear like you've already reached the "confident" zone even if you are not entirely there yet.

Becoming confident does not always happen overnight. As mentioned above, the first step is to change your mindset. The next step is to change your behavior. Here is where the old adage "fake it till you make it" becomes relevant.

If you think and act confidently, soon you will start to unleash the confidence within you. If you are not there yet, you can always fake confidence by trying the following tips:

1. Communicate confidence through body language.

Being sociable isn't always about what you say; it also matters how you present yourself through your movements.

Stop slouching, stop looking down on the floor, and stop fidgeting. All these movements give away how nervous you are. Instead, look at people whom you think are really confident and try to emulate their body language. Practice the following tips everyday even if you are not around other people:

- Stand up straight with your shoulders level and wide; do not fold your arms in front of your chest as it makes you look more closed off and unwilling to engage.

- When sitting down, maintain a good straight posture, and keep your hands relaxed. Keep your back and your neck straight to sit taller.

- When introducing yourself to others, offer a firm handshake and keep eye contact.

- When talking or listening to someone, maintain eye contact about 60-70% of the time and look somewhere else to break the contact, so it does not appear like you are staring.

- Maintain an open body language so you look more approachable. Always make sure your body is facing the person or people you are talking to.

2. Speak clearly in a moderate pace.

It's not about what you say, but the way you say it.

Sure, what you say is important, but if the person you are talking to can't hear or understand you, then it is pointless. So try to speak audibly in just the right volume appropriate for the setting, and the right tone appropriate for what you are saying.

Nervous people tend to mumble and speak faster. So practice speaking at a slower pace, but not too slow that you might bore your listener. Speaking slower makes you seem more confident in what you are saying.

If you find yourself speaking a bit fast, and your listener is struggling to understand you, take a short pause and begin speaking with regular breathing intervals to moderate the speed.

3. Listen to understand.

If you are out in a social situation, wouldn't you want to feel comfortable, relaxed, and valued? That's exactly what everyone else wants.

So when engaging in a conversation, try to make the other person feel comfortable by actually listening to them, and try to understand and imagine what they are describing. This will help you to be more empathetic, and people will like talking to you.

Don't begin rehearsing in your head what you will say in response. Instead, really listen to them so you can understand what they are feeling. You do not always have to say something to make the other person feel like they are heard. The right response will come to you if you feel what they are saying.

Having empathy and making people feel comfortable talking to you will make you seem more confident. More people will gravitate towards you because of the way you make them feel.

In addition, the pressure of carrying the conversation is drastically lessened if you let the other person speak freely while you listen.

Practice Your Confidence

Use it or lose it! So now that you think confidently and you act confidently, it's time for you to go out and try to practice your new found self-confidence. If you don't, you might revert back to your old self-deprecating, insecure tendencies.

You can practice your confidence by actually going out and putting yourself in social situations. However, if you feel you are not ready for that, you can do some practicing with people whom you trust, like your family or close friends. You can try to role-play wherein your friend can act like a stranger at a social event, and you will practice how to introduce yourself and strike up a conversation. Don't forget to ask for feedback so you can continue to improve on your social skills.

You can also ask a friend to go with you in a social event, so you don't feel so vulnerable if you are not yet fully confident to give it a shot on your own.

The point is, the positive self-talk and confident body language can only help you so much. Practicing in real social situations will make sure that you maintain and keep that confidence. It is understandable that you may not feel comfortable about socializing that quickly, so the next chapter will help you begin with next step of the journey, which is to socialize in the real world.

CHAPTER SUMMARY:

- Confidence plays an important role in improving your social skills. If you are confident about yourself, your thoughts, and your actions, you can easily strike up a conversation or join in any discussion.

- To build self-confidence, there are a few tricks you can do. These are: stop negative self-talk, accept yourself as who you are, focus on yourself, and level your expectations.

- Faking confidence helps by making it appear that you are confident and not nervous at all. You can do this by communication through proper body language, speaking at a moderate pace, and listening to understand.

- To effectively establish and maintain self-confidence, you need to practice it in real-life situations and on a regular basis.

Chapter 4: Start Slow but Keep Improving

Practicing in a real social situation will help you strengthen your confidence and further develop your social skills over time.

It is perfectly normal if you are still overwhelmed by the idea of going to a party on your own or asking someone out on a date. If you are shy or introverted by nature, forcing yourself to go big too quickly will only make you more anxious and stressed, and may even lead to heart complications.

So it is advisable to take it one step at a time. It doesn't matter how small the first few steps are; the important thing is you keep moving forward.

Make little improvements every time, and make sure to practice everyday. If you aren't ready for a full blown conversation, start by saying good morning to your neighbors or saying thank you to the cleaning lady. Keep doing this and then next time, try to ask the person sitting next to you on a train a simple question.

Keep making improvements each time. The goal is to overcome your anxiety of interacting with another human being.

Pretty soon, you will be ready to have a casual conversation with a co-worker or a classmate for five minutes. You can try to make the conversation longer and keep them engaged for a longer period each time you practice.

However, an important thing to remember is to mind the quality of your social interactions rather than the quantity. You can say hello to 50 people per day, but keeping a conversation going would still be a challenge. So even if you only practice with a few people, make sure the level and quality of conversation improves every time.

Once you are already comfortable with talking to the same people, maybe you can challenge yourself and go to places you haven't been before, where you don't know anyone. Go to places that interest you and try to strike up a conversation with someone who shares the same interest.

If you are into arts, try to check out the local museum and interact with someone in there. You will already have a good conversation starter, since you have the same interest and there are plenty of interesting pieces in a museum to talk about.

If you are into fitness, go to a gym that you haven't been to before, you will most likely find other people who are into fitness as much as you are.

By taking little steps every time, you can ease yourself into more complex and more challenging social interactions, like going out on a date or attending a corporate event. The next chapter will give you some tips on how to handle yourself in these situations.

* * * * *

CHAPTER SUMMARY:

- Practice makes perfect. It doesn't matter how small the first steps you take are; the more thing is to keep moving forward.

- You can start practicing social confidence by saying good morning to your neighbors or asking about how their day was. The next time you see them, you can probably share about an interesting thing that happened at work.

- Keep making improvements each time. The goal is to overcome your anxiety of interacting with another human being.

Chapter 5: It's Okay to Ask Questions

Asking questions is one of the fundamental elements of interpersonal communication. It serves the purpose of gathering information, clarification of an idea, and it helps you gain control of a conversation.

If you feel uneasy talking about yourself, encourage the other person to talk about themselves, their interests, or their experiences by asking questions. When you ask questions about the other person in the conversation, it conveys the message that you are interested in getting to know them and it makes you appear more empathic and confident.

Asking questions also help you gain insight on the personality of the other person, giving you the opportunity to evaluate how you would carry on a conversation with them.

Furthermore, asking questions will help encourage the flow of thought and ideas, which will make the conversation, go more smoothly. It will also give you plenty more things to talk about, allowing you to prolong the interaction for longer periods of time.

Sounds pretty easy, right? The challenge here is knowing how to ask your questions. Here are some of the things to consider before asking questions in a group or one-on-one social interaction.

1. Figure out what type of question you should ask.

There are a lot of different types of questions. The two main types are closed-ended and open-ended questions.

A close-ended question is answerable by a simple one-word or a single phrase answer. Examples are yes-or-no questions, or questions where you ask a person to choose between two or more choices, or questions that require identifying specific information with a short answer, such as "what time is it?" or "what is your name?"

This type of question is mostly used in the beginning of a conversation or when starting another topic. If you want to find out certain specific information about the person you are talking to, and you don't know how they would respond, start off with a closed-ended question. If they seem dismissive, then you would know not to pursue that conversation. On the other hand, if they start elaborating their responses to a closed-ended question, then you know that they want to engage in a conversation with you.

Open-ended questions require longer responses. You would expect the person to answer with more information and more insight when you ask this type of question. For example "how do you keep a healthy lifestyle?", or "tell me more about your trip to Europe." If you are well into a conversation, and you feel the other person is warming up to you, try asking open-ended questions about themselves to move the interaction further and deeper.

2. Make sure the question is appropriate.

Depending on your purpose, the setting of the conversation and the kind of interpersonal relationship that you have with the other person, you should always make sure that the questions you are asking are appropriate.

If you were strangers who just met, it would be inappropriate to ask questions that are too personal. If you wish to build a network, only ask questions that will help you further your purpose. If you were in the workplace, work-related questions would be more appropriate.

3. Is the timing is right.

Do not just make a list of questions in your mind and just fire away like an interview. Allow the conversation to run its natural course and ask questions regarding what the other person just said. Interject only when the conversation is steering in an unpleasant direction.

If you keep practicing your conversational skills, you will get a better sense of timing. Make sure you are not interrupting the other person's train of thought when you ask the question, so do not ask too many questions too fast.

Once you get used to these things, asking questions would be a breeze. It makes sustaining a conversation so much easier since it takes much of the pressure off of you. However, do remember that a conversation is not a one-way street. Let the other person ask you questions, too, and respond accordingly, instead of just throwing them questions one after another.

✶ ✶ ✶ ✶ ✶

CHAPTER SUMMARY:

- Asking questions is a fundamental element in communication. It helps you acquire more knowledge, get to know the other person better, and start an interesting conversation.

- When asking questions, there are a couple of things you need to keep in mind, such as the type of questions you should ask, how appropriate the questions are, and whether or not the timing is right.

Chapter 6: Go Out and Experience the World

Congratulations for reaching this far!

By now, you must have already practiced a lot, you have learned a lot of topics of conversation and you must feel pretty confident about yourself and your social skills. However, you can still do a lot of things to further improve your socialization.

The last tip is simple: Experience the world and enjoy your life. As the popular saying goes, you only live once (read: Y.O.L.O.), so try new things, meet new people, and make memorable adventures.

Go out and do things that bring you excitement, enjoyment, and happiness. If that's going sky diving, volunteering to build shelter for the underprivileged, watching your favorite artist in a concert, or going on a trip to a place you've never been to, just go for it!

Build on more life experiences that you will be excited to tell your friends or acquaintances about.

The more interesting your life is, the more you'd want to tell a story about it to other people. If your life is boring, on the other hand, you would believe that your thoughts aren't worth listening to, and thus you would shy away from interacting with interesting people.

Here are some ideas I've personally tried that helped me overcome my social fear and improve the way I communicate with other people. Browse through the list and you can maybe get some ideas that you can try out for yourself.

- Sing in front of a crowd.

- Interview a famous personality.

- Do bungee jumping.
- Hike.
- Travel to a different country alone.
- Visit museums, chapels, temples, and interesting architectures.
- Surf.
- Be on TV.
- Camp.
- Prank your friends.
- Prank strangers.
- Do kind deeds to strangers.
- Drive at 140kph on a freeway (Don't forget to wear your seat belt!)
- Join Halloween trick or treat.
- Wear a costume.
- Wear a mascot.
- Write a book.
- Attend a concert.
- Watch a play.
- Tour with your favorite band.
- Join movements with a cause.

- Eat a box of pizza or two by yourself.
- Run a marathon.
- Teach preschool.

And the list goes on.

So, challenge yourself to do something different everyday and tell it to a friend, make a video, or blog about it. The key is to share it to other people and make them feel like they're part of your adventure.

When you realize that your life is interesting and full of excitement, you wouldn't stop telling people about it.

* * * * *

CHAPTER SUMMARY:

- The last and most interesting strategy to overcome your social fear and improve your conversation skills is to live your life to the fullest.

- Do exciting and interesting things that you have never done before. If your life is full of adventures that make you feel alive, you will instinctively feel that desire to share it with the world.

Conclusion

There you have it. Thank you again for downloading this book!

I hope this book was able to help you plan on how you can successfully improve your social skills and prepare yourself for many social situations that you will have to face throughout your life.

The next step is to practice and keep improving. As they say, "slowly but surely". Don't stress yourself too much. The more you think about it, the heavier the pressure you're giving yourself. Just relax, and take the lessons you learned from this book one at a time. Eventually, you will get where you needed to be.

So, go on. Go outside and see the world. People are waiting to hear you speak, because your thoughts matter. You matter.

Finally, if you enjoyed this book, then I'd like to ask you for a favor, would you be kind enough to leave a review for this book on Amazon? It'd be greatly appreciated!

Thank you and good luck!

www.ingramcontent.com/pod-product-compliance
Lightning Source LLC
Chambersburg PA
CBHW030547220526
45463CB00007B/3016